by David Sabino
illustrated by Charles Lehman

Ready-to-Read

SIMON SPOTLIGHT

An imprint of Simon & Schuster Children's Publishing Division
New York   London   Toronto   Sydney   New Delhi
1230 Avenue of the Americas, New York, New York 10020
This Simon Spotlight edition December 2018
Text copyright © 2018 by Simon & Schuster, Inc.
Illustrations copyright © 2018 by Simon & Schuster, Inc.
For information about special discounts for bulk purchases, please contact Simon & Schuster Special Sales at
1-866-506-1949 or business@simonandschuster.com.
Manufactured in the United States of America 1118 LAK
2   4   6   8   10   9   7   5   3   1
Cataloging-in-Publication Data for this title is available from the Library of Congress.
ISBN 978-1-5344-3242-0 (hc)
ISBN 978-1-5344-3241-3 (pbk)
ISBN 978-1-5344-3243-7 (eBook)

GLOSSARY

ACE: A team's best starting pitcher

BALL: A pitch out of the strike zone when the batter does not swing

BALTIMORE CHOP: When a batter intentionally hits a ball downward onto home plate to create a higher bounce during which they can run to first base

BASES LOADED: When runners are on every base

COUNT: The number of balls and strikes during a plate appearance

CYCLE: When a player hits a single, double, triple, and home run in one game

DOUBLE: A hit where the batter reaches second base safely

DOUBLE PLAY: A play in which the fielding team gets two outs on one play

DUGOUT: Covered bench areas down the first and third base lines where teams sit

ERROR: A mistake made by a player on the field that would normally be an out

FOUL BALL: A ball hit outside of the first or third base lines

FULL COUNT: When a batter has three balls and two strikes

GRAND SLAM: A home run hit with the bases loaded that adds four runs to the score

HIT BY PITCH: When the pitch thrown hits the batter, he gets to go to first base

HOME RUN: A hit during which the batter runs around all the bases to score a run

INNING: The basic unit of play that consists of two halves or frames, the "top" (first half) and the "bottom" (second half). In each half one team bats until three outs are made, with the other team playing defense. The home team plays the bottom half of the frame.

LEADOFF: The first batter in a game or an inning

NO-HITTER: A game in which no batter on a team reaches a base safely by getting a hit

PERFECT GAME: A game in which the pitcher gets every batter on the opposing team out

POP-UP: A ball hit in the air that does not reach the outfield

RELIEVER: A pitcher who enters a game to replace another pitcher

RUN: When a base runner safely reaches home plate

RUN BATTED IN (RBI): A hit that results in a run being scored

SEVENTH INNING STRETCH: The time between the top and bottom of the seventh inning, during which everyone, including the fans and the players, takes a quick break

SINGLE: A hit where the batter reaches first base safely

STRIKE: A pitch thrown in the strike zone, or swung at and missed by the batter

STRIKEOUT: When a batter gets three strikes and his turn at bat is over

STRIKE ZONE: The area over home plate between the batter's knees and chest, as well as the right and left edges of home plate

STOLEN BASE: When a runner advances on a pitch without a ball being hit into play

TRIPLE: A hit where the batter reaches third base safely

WALK: When a batter gets four balls and is allowed to "walk" to first base

WORLD SERIES: Major League Baseball's championship round in which the first team to win four out of seven games becomes the World Series champion

It's a beautiful day.
Are you ready to watch
a baseball game?
Great! Let's go!

Hello! My name is Lily.
I'm the announcer at this
Major League Baseball stadium.
I tell the fans what's
going on in the game.

In the United States baseball
is called the national pastime.
That means lots of people
like to play it and watch it!

WiN

Historians believe the
first baseball game
was played more than
two hundred years ago.
Today the Bluebirds are playing
against the Mavericks.
Let's watch everyone prepare
for the game.

HOT
DOG

HOT
DOG

POP
CORN

GO!

GO

Here is the press box.
This is where I work!
I can see all the action
on the field from here.

I announce which players are
coming up to bat.
Sometimes I get to wish fans
happy birthday!

Now let's go down to the field
to meet the players!
There are six players in
the infield and three players
in the outfield.

Home plate is at one corner
of the diamond, and the bases
are on the other three.
Batters stand next to home plate
when they try to hit the ball.
Players run ninety feet to get from
one base to the next.

If a player hits a ball and
runs to first base,
that's called a single.
If he runs to second, it's
a double. If he runs to third,
it's a triple.

If he hits the ball over the fence
or manages to run all the way
home without getting
thrown out, it's a home run!

Before every game two
white foul lines are drawn
by the groundskeeper.
He uses a machine called a
field striper.

Most of them have big wheels
that roll chalk or paint along
the grass and dirt.

If a player hits a ball and it lands
outside of these lines,
it's called a foul ball.

A ball hit inside of the lines
is called a fair ball.

Oliver is the catcher for
the Mavericks.
He squats behind home plate.
Oliver wears a special mask,
glove, and padding to
help keep him safe.

The area where pitchers get ready
is called the bullpen.
Tommy, the pitcher, warms up
by playing catch with Oliver.
Tommy throws softly at first, but
after a while he'll throw harder
and harder until the game starts.

Together the pitcher and catcher
are known as the battery.
The catcher helps the pitcher
choose what pitch to throw by
giving the pitcher signs.

To have the pitcher throw a fastball, the catcher might show one finger. Two fingers often means a curveball. Sometimes the pitcher wants to throw a different pitch from what the catcher suggests.

If the pitcher doesn't want to throw
what the catcher suggests, he will
shake his head and wait for another
sign. It's important that the catcher
keeps all the signs hidden, so
the batter doesn't know what
pitch is coming.

During the game Tommy pitches
from the pitching mound.
That's the raised circle of dirt
in the middle of the diamond.
The mound is located
sixty feet and six inches away
from home plate.

There's a rectangle in the middle
of the mound called
the pitching rubber.
Pitchers must have their foot
on the rubber to throw
a legal pitch.

Rick is about to take
batting practice.
He is rubbing pine tar on his bat
to help him grip it.

The first and third basemen play close to their bases. The shortstop and second baseman move around slightly between the bases in order to be in a good position to catch any balls the batter hits.

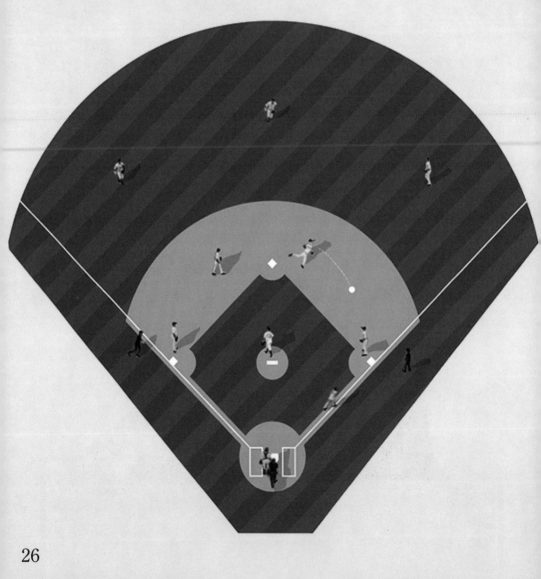

The left fielder, center fielder,
and right fielder
play in the outfield.
Their job is to catch
the balls that are hit far
and throw them back quickly.

Lots of fans show up early
for batting practice, hoping
to get autographs from
the players.

There are four umpires in
every game: one at home plate
and one at each base.
They are not connected
to any team. The home-plate umpire
decides whether each pitch
is a ball or a strike.

If a batter gets three strikes,
he is out and his turn is over.
If he gets four balls, he goes to
first base. Each team gets
three outs in each inning.

Baseball games are usually
nine innings long, but if the score
is tied at the end of the
ninth inning, the teams keep playing
until one team wins.
There is no time limit.

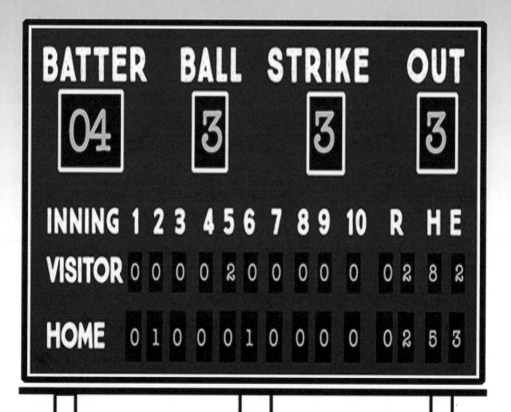

BATTER	BALL	STRIKE	OUT
04	3	3	3

INNING	1	2	3	4	5	6	7	8	9	10	R	H	E
VISITOR	0	0	0	0	2	0	0	0	0	0	2	8	2
HOME	0	1	0	0	0	1	0	0	0	0	2	5	3

The game is about to begin!
The Mavericks run onto the field.
I say all their names over
the loudspeaker. Next the
national anthem is played.
I introduce the first batter
for the Bluebirds.

Tommy is on the pitcher's mound.
Oliver squats behind home plate.
He puts down one finger.
Tommy knows that is the sign
for a fastball and nods.
He winds up and throws
the first pitch.
Let's play ball!

You don't have to go to the stadium to know what happens at a baseball game. Lots of people all over the world listen to baseball games on the radio or watch on television. You can read about baseball in newspapers and on websites. And of course you can always play baseball with your friends and have lots of fun! Keep reading to learn some fun facts every serious baseball fan should know.

TEN COOL FACTS ABOUT BASEBALL

1. The Boston Americans won the first World Series in 1903. They are now called the Boston Red Sox.

2. "Take Me Out to the Ball Game" is often heard at games during the seventh-inning stretch. That happens between the top and bottom of the seventh inning. The songwriters had never attended a game when they wrote it in 1908!

3. Fans eat about twenty million hot dogs per year at Major League Baseball games. That's equal to about eight thousand per game.

4. The youngest player to appear in the major leagues was fifteen-year-old Joe Nuxhall, who began his career in 1944. He played for the Cincinnati Reds.

5. The distance of running around the bases during a home run is the same as running from the back of one end zone to the other on a football field (360 feet).

6. In 1989 Deion Sanders hit a home run for the New York Yankees and scored a touchdown for the Atlanta Falcons football team in the same week!

7. Cal Ripken of the Baltimore Orioles went sixteen years without missing a game. He played in 2,632 straight games from 1982 to 1998.

8. In 1999 St. Louis Cardinals player Fernando Tatis became the only player to ever hit two grand slam home runs in the same inning! Amazingly, both came off of the same Los Angeles Dodgers pitcher, Chan Ho Park.

9. Some fun names of Minor League Baseball teams include the Akron Rubber Ducks, Binghamton Rumble Ponies, Hartford Yard Goats, New Orleans Baby Cakes, and Vermont Lake Monsters.

10. Baseball will return to the Olympics in 2020. It was an Olympic sport from 1992 until 2008. The country of Cuba has won the most baseball gold medals with three.

AND EVEN MORE FACTS!

1. In 2010 Cincinnati Reds pitcher Aroldis Chapman threw the fastest pitch ever recorded in baseball. The ball traveled 105.1 miles per hour and took less than half of one second to reach home plate!

2. On August 22, 2007, the Texas Rangers scored thirty runs in one game against the Baltimore Orioles. That is the most runs scored by any team in any Major League Baseball game in more than 120 years.

3. The longest game in Major League Baseball history was between the Chicago White Sox and Milwaukee Brewers in 1984. It took eight hours and six minutes and twenty-five innings for the White Sox to win, 7–6.

4. In 1919 the New York Giants beat the Philadelphia Phillies, 6–1. It took just fifty-one minutes. That's still the shortest game in Major League Baseball history.

5. The Brooklyn Robins (later called the Dodgers) and Boston Braves played the most innings in a major league game. The teams played twenty-six innings before calling their 1920 game a tie, 1–1. That's nearly the length of three regular games (twenty-seven innings)!

6. Mud is applied to brand-new baseballs before packaging them and shipping them to all the baseball teams in the major leagues. The mud is applied because brand-new baseballs are much too slick for pitchers to grip properly. The mud comes from a secret spot in southern New Jersey off of the Delaware River. The tradition of rubbing this special mud into balls started in 1938 and continues to this day.